Rainbow Nest

by Edyta Sitar

Landauer Publishing, LLC

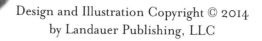

Design and Illustration Copyright © 2014
by Landauer Publishing, LLC

Text and Project Copyright© 2013
by Edyta Sitar
This book was designed, produced, and published
by Landauer Publishing, LLC
3100 101st Street, Urbandale, IA 50322
800-557-2144; 515-287-2144; landauerpub.com

President/Publisher: Jeramy Lanigan Landauer
Vice President of Sales and Administration: Kitty Jacobson
Editor: Jeri Simon
Art Director: Laurel Albright
Photographer: Sue Voegtlin
Illustrator: Sue Cornelison

This book is printed on acid-free paper.

Printed in Mexico: 10 9 8 7 6 5 4 3 2 1

Library of Congress Control Number: 2014942381

ISBN 13: 978-1-935726-55-5

Dedication

For My Children

Delfina, Anna and Michael—
you are my inspiration and my joy.

As the earth wakes up
from beneath the snow,
Mama prepares for a
new spring arrival.

She sees the leaves turn green outside the window, where Chelsea the chickadee is busy pecking at a nest of moss and sticks while dreaming of her babies' happy chirps:

"Chick-a-dee-dee! Chick-a-dee-dee!".

Before baby comes, Mama has things to do.

Snip, snip!

go the sounds of her sewing scissors,
as fabrics fall like a rainbow of colors. Blue, red,
green and yellow come floating down as tiny pieces
of fabric sprinkle the floor.

Chhk, chhk! Snip, snip!

And snip some more.

The tiniest cutaway scraps cling tight in happy hugs and hopeful wishes that baby will someday play among them.

Pitter Patter! Pitter Patter!

Go the sounds of Mama's feet
as she sweeps up the scattered rainbow.

Swish, swish!

Goes the broom as it sweeps away
the fabric flakes into a dustpan, out the
door, and into a basket of colors.

With a gust of wind—*swoosh!*—
and a tad of spring magic,
the air grabs those colorful fabric flakes.
Swirling and swaying as if dancing in the trees,
the pieces flutter gently within Chelsea's reach.

"Coo-coo!"
Chelsea says to welcome
the finds that will fluff
her cozy nest.

Inside, Mama pieces and stitches her rainbow together.

Pop!

goes her needle as it pokes through fabric layers.

Wirrhhh!

goes the thread as it sings its own spring song.

Pop! in and out,

Wirrhhh! up and down,

Pop! in and out,

Wirrhhh! up and down.

In a moment of rest, Mama looks through the glass to see Chelsea finishing her rainbow nest. There in the middle of the grass and moss, nestled among the brightly colored fabric bits, are three speckled eggs resting oh-so quietly!

Shhhh!

Then tap, tap, tap! "Who's there?" wonders Chelsea.

"Knock-knock! Knock-knock!

Pickety-poke! Pickety-poke!"

From each of the eggs peeks a tiny baby beak.

Out come curious wet and wobbly heads...
then three chirping little babies all
trying their voices for the very first time.

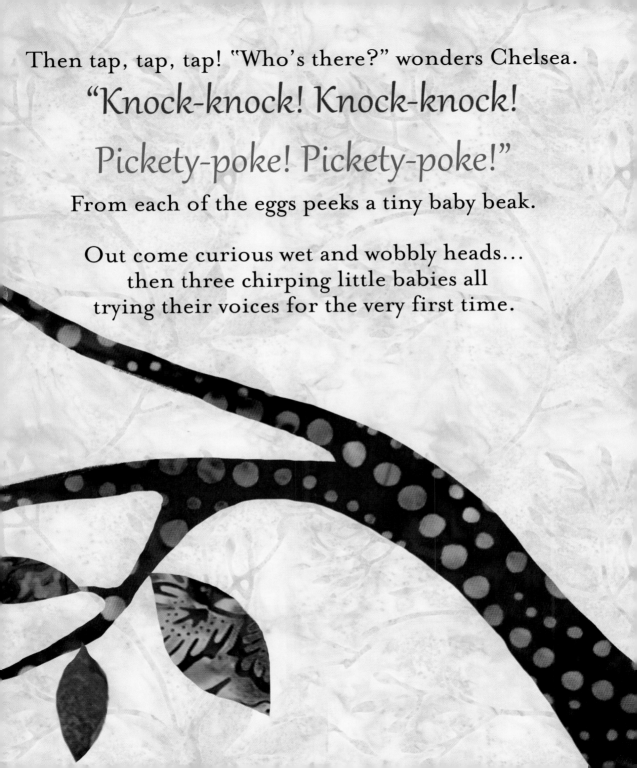

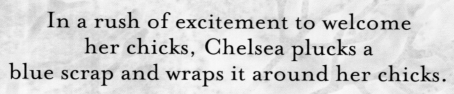

In a rush of excitement to welcome
her chicks, Chelsea plucks a
blue scrap and wraps it around her chicks.

"Chick-a-dee-dee! Chick-a-dee-dee!"

the babies chirp with delight, as they cuddle
with Chelsea in their rainbow nest.

Inside, Mama is busy just the same——
playing and loving her own newly arrived chickadee.

Cuddled in the rainbow quilt that Mama stitched with
love, her little baby is a lucky bird.

Rainbow Nest

39" Square

Rainbow Nest Quilt

Materials

2 yards total light print fabrics for background square, blocks and B squares

24—10" squares in a variety of medium-to-dark batiks for blocks, binding and straw appliqués

Note: In the quilt shown, blocks are assembled using medium-to-dark batiks from four main color families— blue, brown, green and red. There are approximately 18 blocks from each color family.

10" square dark brown batik for branch appliqué

4 assorted 4" x 6" rectangles brown batiks for nest and bird appliqués

4 assorted 5" squares green batiks for leaf appliqués

4" square turquoise batik for egg appliqués

2-1/2 yards backing fabric

45" square batting

Finished appliqué block: 15" square
Finished quilt: 39" square

Quantities are for 44/45"-wide, 100% cotton fabrics. Measurements include 1/4" seam allowances. Sew with right sides together unless otherwise stated.

Cut the Fabrics

From light print fabrics, cut:

1 — 17" background square

Note: The background square is cut 1-1/2" larger than required. This allows you to trim your block to size after the appliqué is complete.

72 — 3-1/2" B squares

288 — 1-1/2" A squares

From *each* medium-to-dark batik, cut:

1—2-1/2"-wide strip to make 180" of binding

360 — 1-1/2" A squares from 20 of the medium-to-dark batiks (approximately 18 from each square)

From backing fabric, cut:

2 — 23" x 45" rectangles

Cut and Assemble the Appliqué Block

1. Trace the appliqué patterns on pages 29-30. Prepare the appliqué pieces using the appliqué method of your choice.

From dark brown batik, cut:

1 pattern A (branch)

From brown batiks, cut:

1 pattern B (nest back)
1 pattern C (nest front)
1 pattern D (bird)
1 pattern E (wing)

From green batiks, cut:

9 pattern F (large leaf)
5 pattern G (medium leaf)
6 pattern H (small leaf)

From turquoise batik, cut:

3 pattern I (egg)

From assorted medium-to-dark

batik scraps, cut:

11 pattern J (straw)

2. Referring to the illustration below, and Placement Diagram on page 31, position the appliqué pieces on the 17" light print background square. Appliqué the shapes in place using your favorite method. A raw edge appliqué technique was used in the Rainbow Nest Quilt. Press the appliquéd block from the back. Center and trim it to 15-1/2" square.

Assemble the Nine-Patch Blocks

1. Referring to Nine-Patch Block Assembly Diagram, lay out five medium-to-dark batik A squares from the same color family and four light print A squares in three rows. **Note**: Refer to the photo on page 26 for color placement ideas. The fabrics in the five medium-to-dark A squares vary from block to block. Sometimes the block has one batik and other times as many as five.

Nine-Patch Block Assembly Diagram

2. Sew the squares in each row together. Press seams toward medium-to-dark A squares.

3. Join the rows to make a Nine-Patch block. Press seams in one direction. Make 72 Nine-Patch blocks.

Make 72

Assemble the Quilt Top

1. Referring to the Quilt Top Assembly Diagram, lay out 72 Nine-Patch blocks and 72 B squares around the appliqué block as shown.

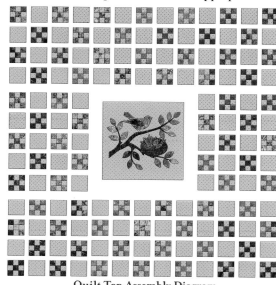

Quilt Top Assembly Diagram

2. Sew the blocks and B squares together in rows. Press seams toward the B squares.

3. Join the short rows to make the side sections. Join the long rows to make the top and bottom sections as shown.

4. Sew the side sections to the appliqué block. Sew the top and bottom sections to the remaining sides of the appliqué block to complete the quilt top.

Complete the Quilt

1. Sew the 23" x 45" backing rectangles together along one long edge, using a 1/2" seam allowance. Press the seam allowance open.
2. Layer the quilt top, batting and pieced backing. Quilt as desired.
3. Bind with medium-to-dark batik binding strips.

THESE SHAPES HAVE BEEN REVERSED
FOR FUSIBLE APPLIQUÉ

RAINBOW
NEST
TEMPLATES

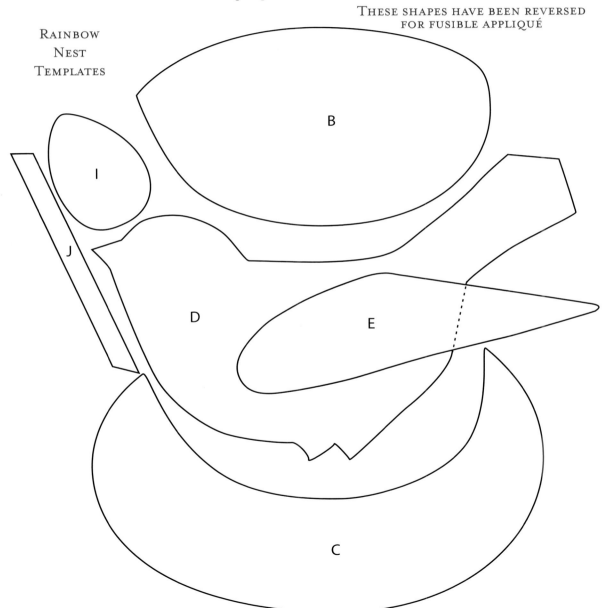

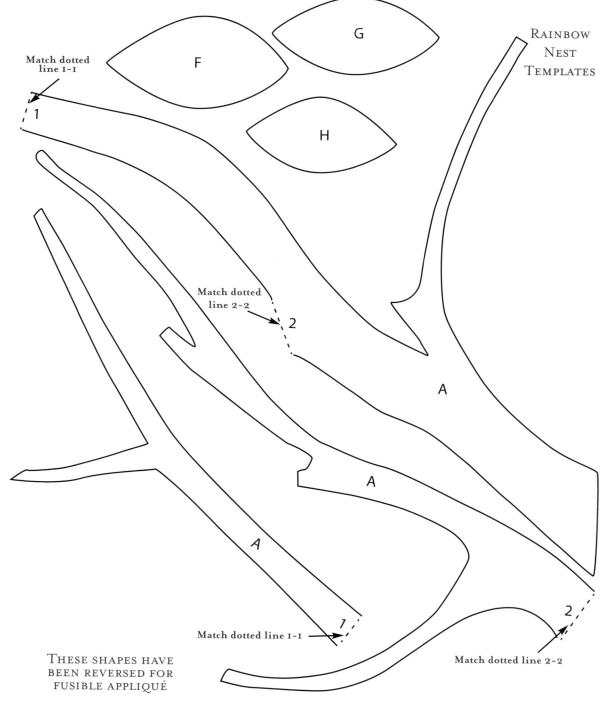

RAINBOW
NEST
TEMPLATES

F

G

H

Match dotted
line 1-1

1

Match dotted
line 2-2

2

A

A

A

Match dotted line 1-1

1

2

Match dotted line 2-2

THESE SHAPES HAVE
BEEN REVERSED FOR
FUSIBLE APPLIQUÉ

Fabric
Marker Details

- - - - Overlay Lines

PLACEMENT DIAGRAM

About the Author

Edyta Sitar is proud to carry on a family tradition that fabric and threads have stitched together through the generations.

Her true love of quilting shines through as she travels the world sharing her passion, connecting to and inspiring quilters of all skill levels with stimulating stories about the quilts she makes. As the owner and co-founder of Laundry Basket Quilts, her work has been published in books and magazines worldwide.

Edyta resides in Marshall, Michigan with her husband and children. There she creates her beautiful, award-winning quilts and patterns and her splendid fabric designs for MODA.

In *Rainbow Nest*, with special thanks to writer Judy Friedman and illustrator Sue Cornelison, Edyta introduces quilters to a story-to-read and a quilt-to-make in anticipation of baby's birth.

About the Illustrator

Sue Cornelison is an award-winning illustrator whose clients include children's publishers *American Girl, Disney Hyperion, Cricket Magazine, Crayola Kids Magazine* and many more.

Sue lives in St. Charles, Iowa with her husband Ross, a jazz musician. Together they have raised six children. Her daughter Molly follows in her mother's footsteps and together they created the illustrations for *Rainbow Nest*.